Mammal
Body Parts

Clare Lewis

heinemann
raintree

D1361272

© 2016 Heinemann-Raintree
an imprint of Capstone Global Library, LLC
Chicago, Illinois

To contact Capstone Global Library please call 800-747-4992, or visit our web site www.capstonepub.com

Edited by Helen Cox Cannons and Shelly Lyons
Designed by Steve Mead
Picture research by Svetlana Zhurkin
Production by Victoria Fitzgerald
Originated by Capstone Global Library Ltd

Library of Congress Cataloging-in-Publication Data
Lewis, Clare, 1976- author.
  Mammal body parts / Clare Lewis.
     pages cm.—(Animal body parts)
Includes bibliographical references and index.
  ISBN 978-1-4846-2552-1 (hb)—ISBN 978-1-4846-2559-0 (pb)—ISBN 978-1-4846-2573-6 (ebook) 1.
Mammals—Anatomy—Juvenile literature. I. Title.

QL739.L49 2016
599—dc23   2014043980

This book has been officially leveled by using the F&P Text Level Gradient™ Leveling System.

Acknowledgments
We would like to thank the following for permission to reproduce photographs: Getty Images: Visuals Unlimited/Ken Catania, 11, Visuals Unlimited/Thomas Marent, 15; Newscom: Photoshot/NHPA/Martin Harvey, 19, Photoshot/NHPA/Nigel Dennis, 22 (middle); Shutterstock: Albie Venter, 16, Asmus, 12, atiger, 4, CreativeNature.nl, 7, Dean Bertoncelj, 23 (top), Dr. Alan Lipkin, 18, Eric Isselee, cover (top middle), Ivan Kuzmin, 22 (bottom), jurra8, cover (top left), Liudmyla Soloviova, cover (bottom), MarclSchauer, cover (top right), Matej Hudovernik, 6, 23, Maxim Petrichuk, 5, Monika Gniot, 13, Patrick Rolands, 17, 23, Paul Banton, 10, Pavel Kovacs, 21, Petro Perutskyi, 23 (grub), Rafal Cichawa, back cover (left), 9, re_bekka, 14, Stephan Morris, 8, 23, Steve Bower, 22 (top), tratong, back cover (right), 20, 23.

We would like to thank Michael Bright for his invaluable help in the preparation of this book.

Printed in the United States of America.
092019   002713

Contents

Some words are shown in bold, **like this**. You can
find out what they mean by looking in the glossary.

What Is a Mammal?

Mammals are animals that have hair or fur. Mammal mothers feed babies their milk.

Dogs and humans are mammals. Whales are mammals that live in the sea.

Mammals do not all look the same.
Their bodies can be very different from
each other.

Let's take a look at parts of their bodies.

Eyes

Mammals have two eyes. Some animals have eyes on the fronts of their heads.

This tarsier has very large eyes to see in the dark. Tarsiers are **nocturnal**.

Many mammals, such as this mouse, have eyes on the sides of their heads.

The mouse's eyes help it to see all around. It can look out for danger.

Ears

Many mammals have very good hearing.

Cats can move their ears one at a time. This movement helps the cat know where sounds are coming from.

Elephants have huge ears. They can hear sounds from very far away. Elephants also flap their ears to help keep them cool.

Noses

Mammals use their noses to help them find food. They also use them to sniff out danger.

Bears have a very good sense of smell.

Star-nosed moles live underground. They have special feelers on their nose to find their way around.

Teeth

Some mammals, such as lions and wolves, eat meat.

This wolf has sharp, pointed teeth for catching **prey** and knife-like teeth for cutting it up.

Mammals that eat plants have large, flat teeth at the back. Flat teeth are good for crushing tough leaves and grasses.

Cows have 32 teeth. They need to eat lots of grass to make their milk.

Tails

Most mammals have tails.

This zebra keeps flies away by hitting them with its tail.

This spider monkey has a long, strong tail.

The monkey uses its tail like a hand to grasp branches.

Legs

antelope

Many mammals have four legs.

Antelopes' long legs help them run away from lions.

seal

Some mammals move well in water. They do not need to move well on land.

Seals, whales, and dolphins have **flippers**. They use their flippers to swim.

Feet and Hands

Some mammals, such as cats and bears, have paws and claws. Claws are good for catching **prey** and for climbing.

This mountain goat has hooves. Hooves are good for climbing on rocks.

chimps

Monkeys, apes, and humans are very good at grasping and holding things. Our thumbs can move separately from our fingers.

Whiskers and Spines

Many mammals have whiskers. Whiskers are thick, stiff hairs.

Meerkats use their whiskers for feeling their way around their underground **burrows**.

Hedgehogs and porcupines have stiff, spiny hairs on their backs.

The hairs help to keep them safe from **predators**.

Totally Amazing Mammal Body Parts!

Armadillos have tough shells as well as hair. The shell on their backs protects them from **predators**.

The aye-aye is a lemur. It has a very long finger on each hand. It uses this finger to hook out **grubs** from tree trunks.

Bats are the only mammals with wings. Flying squirrels have flaps of skin that help them glide between trees.

Glossary

 **burrow** underground home of an animal

 **flipper** wide, flat limb used for swimming

 **grub** young of an insect such as a beetle

 **nocturnal** animal that hunts for food at night and sleeps in the day

 **predator** animal that hunts other animals for food

 **prey** animal that is hunted by another animal

Find Out More

Books

Gray, Susan Heinrichs. *The Life Cycle of Mammals* (Life Cycles). Chicago: Heinemann Library, 2012.

Royston, Angela. *Mammals* (Animal Classifications). Chicago: Heinemann Library, 2015.

Web sites

Facthound offers a safe, fun way to find Internet sites related to this book. All of the sites on Facthound have been researched by our staff.

Here's all you do:
Visit www.facthound.com
Type in this code: 9781484625521

Index